EDGE
BOOKS™

BLOODIEST BATTLES

300 HEROES

THE BATTLE OF THERMOPYLAE

BY TERRI DOUGHERTY

CONSULTANT:
Tim Solie
Adjunct Professor of History
Minnesota State University, Mankato

Capstone
press®
Mankato, Minnesota

Edge Books are published by Capstone Press,
151 Good Counsel Drive, P.O. Box 669, Mankato, Minnesota 56002.
www.capstonepress.com

Library of Congress Cataloging-in-Publication Data
Dougherty, Terri.
    300 heroes : the battle of Thermopylae / by Terri Dougherty.
    p. cm. — (Edge books. Bloodiest battles)
    Includes bibliographical references and index.
    Summary: "Describes events before, during, and after the
Battle of Thermopylae, including key players, weapons, and battle
tactics" — Provided by publisher.
    ISBN-13: 978-1-4296-2296-7 (hardcover)
    ISBN-10: 1-4296-2296-2 (hardcover)
    1. Thermopylae, Battle of, Greece, 480 B.C. — Juvenile literature.
2. Greece — History — Persian Wars, 500–449 B.C. — Juvenile literature.
3. Thermopylae (Greece) — History, Military — Juvenile literature.
I. Title. II. Title: Three hundred heroes. III. Title: Battle of Thermopylae.
IV. Series.
DF225.5.D68 2009
938'.03 — dc22   2008022883

Editorial Credits
Aaron Sautter, editor; Bob Lentz, set designer; Kim Brown,
    book designer/illustrator; Jo Miller, photo researcher

Photo Credits
akg-images, 4
Alamy/North Wind Picture Archives, 14, 15, 18; Peter Oshkai, 29
Corbis/Bettmann, 9, 10
Getty Images Inc./Hulton Archive, 25
The Granger Collection, New York, cover
Mary Evans Picture Library, 12–13, 26; Douglas McCarthy, 22

1 2 3 4 5 6 14 13 12 11 10 09

TABLE OF CONTENTS

CHAPTER 1

THE BRAVE 300

King Leonidas and 300 Spartan warriors fought to defend Greece from the huge Persian Army at Thermopylae.

The ground shuddered as thousands of Persian soldiers marched toward Thermopylae, Greece. But King Leonidas, 300 Spartan warriors, and about 4,000 Greek soldiers were ready to defend their country at any cost.

The Spartans were hardened warriors. They had trained since boyhood. Rows of Spartan fighters stood shoulder to shoulder. They gripped their spears and shields as the mighty Persian Army neared.

Leonidas' soldiers were greatly outnumbered. The Greeks faced tens of thousands of Persian soldiers. They knew they couldn't win. However, they refused to retreat.

The Spartans had some success at first. But they were eventually overwhelmed. As the end of the battle neared, their spears and swords were broken and lost. The warriors kept fighting with their bare hands. They fought to the death to hold off the Persian Army.

In spite of the loss, the Spartans' bravery gave hope to Greece. The Greek people realized they might have a chance for victory. The Spartans' brave act changed the course of history.

Persia versus Greece

The Persian **Empire** was one of the most powerful empires in history. It lasted from around 550 BC to 330 BC. It covered more than 1 million square miles (2.5 million square kilometers). It stretched from Macedonia to Iran and into Egypt. About 70 million people lived in the Persian Empire.

Greece was a small country. It covered only about 50,000 square miles (129,500 square kilometers). When Persia invaded in 480 BC, Greece had less than 2 million people. Greece did not have a central government. Instead, it was made up of a number of **city-states**. Athens and Sparta were the most powerful of the Greek city-states.

NORTH SEA

empire — a group of countries that have the same ruler

city-state — a city in ancient Greece that governed itself

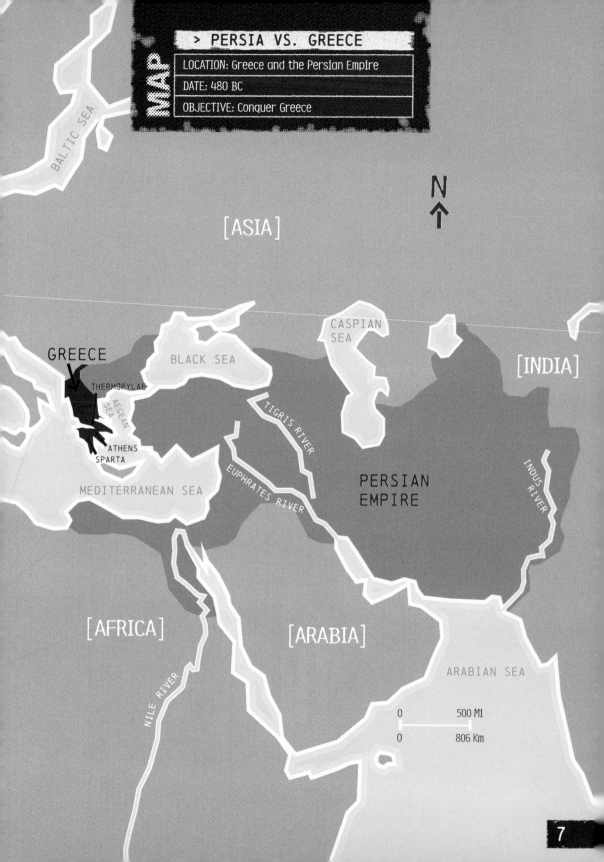

Before the Invasion

The Persians first tried to **invade** Greece in 490 BC. They failed. When Xerxes became king of the Persian Empire, he was determined to finally rule Greece. He gathered a huge army of about 200,000 soldiers to invade the tiny country.

It was Xerxes' custom to give his enemies the chance to surrender before a battle. When his army met the Spartans at Thermopylae, Xerxes' messengers told the Spartans to lay down their weapons. They refused. King Leonidas told the Persian messengers that Xerxes would have to "come and take them."

invade — to send armed forces into another country to take it over

Xerxes became king of Persia in 485 BC.

CHAPTER 2

PREPARING FOR BATTLE

King Leonidas bravely led the Spartans into a fight they couldn't win.

The Greeks knew the Persian Army was coming. But not all Greeks were sure they wanted to fight. Each city-state had its own government and its own way of doing things. Some wanted to surrender rather than be killed. Others didn't want to fight because a religious festival was to be held soon.

King Leonidas knew the battle would be deadly. Yet he didn't back down. He gathered 300 of the best Spartan soldiers to fight with him. He took only men who had living sons. If his men were killed, Leonidas wanted their family lines to continue.

King Leonidas knew the Persian Army was huge and powerful. He knew that they couldn't win. Yet he willingly went into battle with just 300 Spartans and about 4,000 other Greek troops.

FACT:

> GUIDED BY RELIGION

Religion was important to the Greeks. Before facing Persia, Leonidas visited the Greek Oracle. It was believed this religious leader could see into the future. The Oracle said that Greece would either lose a king in battle, or be overrun by the Persians.

Persian Forces

Persia's soldiers came from the countries the empire had already captured. Soldiers wore battle gear from their homelands. Some had helmets and carried long knives or battle axes. Others fought from a distance with bows and arrows. Some soldiers wore fish-scale armor. Many carried daggers on their belts. Most soldiers dressed lightly, so they could attack with speed. The Persian Army also had a **cavalry**.

cavalry — soldiers who travel and fight on horseback

Xerxes' huge army had thousands of soldiers from across the Persian Empire.

King Xerxes had a **guard** of 10,000 specially trained warriors. They were called the Immortals. The Immortals wore uniforms woven with gold. Their spears had silver blades. The Immortals carried wicker shields. A bow and quiver of arrows was slung over their shoulders. The Immortals were famous for their fierce fighting. They had never been defeated.

guard — a group of soldiers who protect an important person or place

The Spartans

Spartans warriors began training for battle at a young age. A Spartan boy's education stressed discipline, courage, and skill. As adults, Spartan men spent their time training or fighting. They were extremely loyal to their country. Little was more important than being a good Spartan citizen.

Spartan soldiers fought on foot. They wore helmets and armor made of bronze. They also carried shields made of bronze and wood. Spartan warriors fought with swords and long spears. They believed that fighting battles with bows and arrows was a sign of weakness.

Spartan armor and weapons were made mostly from bronze.

The Spartan Army used advanced methods of fighting. Eight rows of soldiers stood shoulder to shoulder. Each soldier protected the men fighting on either side of him. Soldiers overlapped their shields in front of them to create a wall called a **phalanx**. The phalanx protected them while they pierced their enemies with spears. If a soldier's spear broke, he fought with his double-edged sword. These methods made the Spartans very effective in battle.

phalanx — a protective wall soldiers made by overlapping their shields

Greek Strategy

King Leonidas knew the Persians would have to travel through a small strip of land to invade Greece. This narrow mountain pass was called Thermopylae. It had a tall mountain ridge on one side. A high cliff overlooked the sea on the other side.

Leonidas believed this pass was the perfect place to fight the Persian Army. Because it was so narrow, only a few soldiers could get through at a time. The Persian Army's great numbers would be easier to handle there.

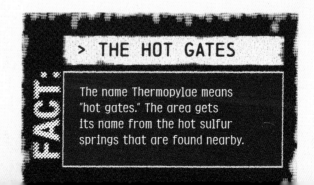

> **THE HOT GATES**

The name Thermopylae means "hot gates." The area gets its name from the hot sulfur springs that are found nearby.

FACT

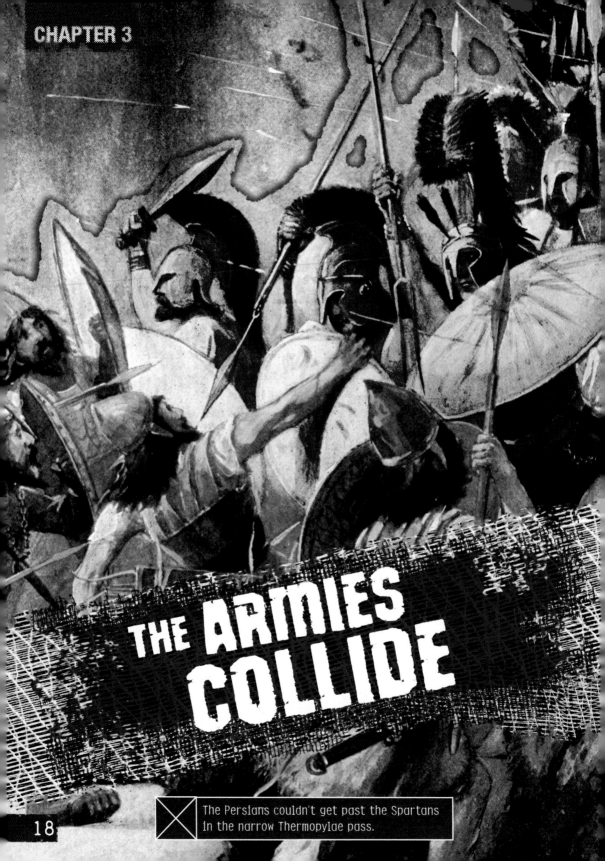

CHAPTER 3

THE ARMIES COLLIDE

The Persians couldn't get past the Spartans in the narrow Thermopylae pass.

The Spartans were ready when the first Persian warriors attacked. Their spears easily pierced the Persians' light armor. But Xerxes' army was gigantic. Wave after wave of Persian warriors charged the Spartans. For every Persian soldier who fell, another took his place. Soon, dead soldiers lay everywhere. It was impossible to keep fighting. The battered Persians had to stop the attack to remove the dead.

King Xerxes then decided to send in his best forces — the Immortals. But even they couldn't overwhelm the Spartans. The Spartans were clever fighters who knew how to trick their enemies. They fooled the Persians by turning and pretending to retreat. When the enemy followed them into the narrow pass, the Spartans turned on them and fought fiercely. By the end of the day, 10,000 Persian soldiers were dead.

FACT:

> AN IMPOSSIBLE MISSION

A Greek spy reported that the Persians had so many archers their arrows could "blot out the sun." One Spartan replied, "So much the better - we shall fight them in the shade."

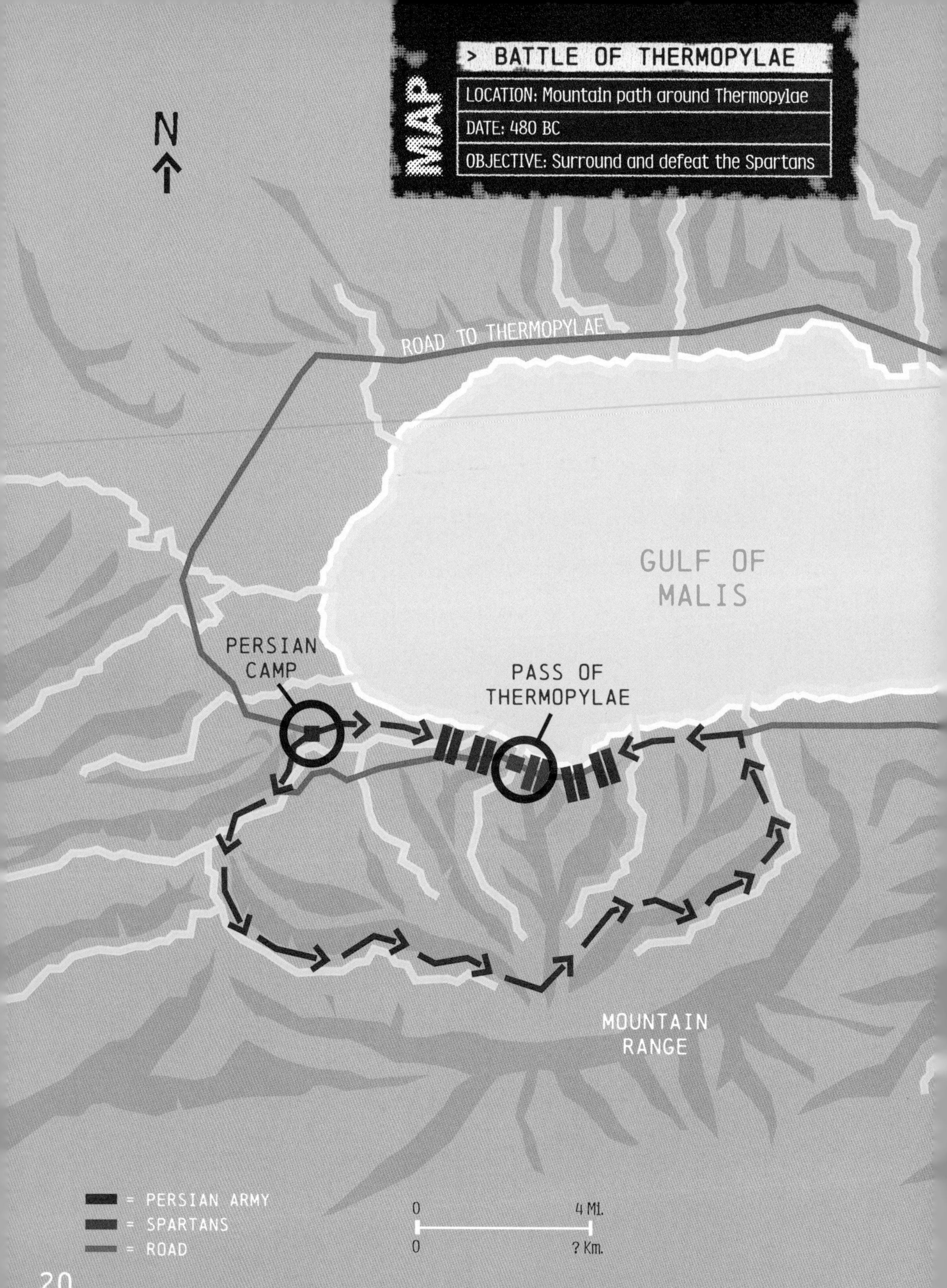

MAP
> BATTLE OF THERMOPYLAE
LOCATION: Mountain path around Thermopylae
DATE: 480 BC
OBJECTIVE: Surround and defeat the Spartans
N
ROAD TO THERMOPYLAE
GULF OF MALIS
PERSIAN CAMP
PASS OF THERMOPYLAE
MOUNTAIN RANGE
= PERSIAN ARMY
= SPARTANS
= ROAD
0
4 Mi.
0
? Km.

Betrayed

The battle raged throughout the next day. But the Spartans still held off the Persians. King Xerxes was furious. His troops couldn't get through the pass. He sent messengers to ask nearby villagers if there was another way over the mountain. He promised a reward for helpful information.

Most Greeks who lived in the area wouldn't help the Persian soldiers. But one man named Ephialtes chose to **betray** the Greeks. He was greedy and thought he would receive a large reward. He told Xerxes about a path that wound around and over the mountains. The path ended at a spot behind the Greeks. Ephialtes said he would lead Xerxes' forces over the path in return for gold.

Xerxes quickly agreed. That night, he sent his best soldiers over the path. The full moon lit the way as 10,000 Immortals crept around the Greek soldiers.

betray — to do something that is not loyal

The Spartans wanted to look and perform their best for their final battle.

The End Nears

During the night, King Leonidas learned that the Persians were heading over the mountain path. He knew his small army would soon be defeated. He ordered most of the Greek soldiers to retreat. He wanted them to be able to fight for Greece another day. But Leonidas stayed behind with the 300 Spartans and about 1,700 other Greek soldiers. He wanted to give the retreating soldiers a chance to get away.

In the morning, Leonidas told his troops to eat a hearty breakfast. He knew it would be their last meal. The Spartans got ready for their last battle by exercising and combing their long hair. They also rubbed oil on their bodies. They knew they were about to die, but they weren't afraid. They were preparing to fight and die an honorable death.

The Last Stand

The Greek warriors moved outside the pass to face the Persians for the last time. The Persians showered them with arrows. Soon, the Greeks were completely surrounded. But they surged forward so strongly that some Persians were trampled.

However, the Greeks were soon overwhelmed. The Spartans' battle formation fell apart. They no longer had the phalanx to protect them. They were forced to fight the Persians in hand-to-hand combat. When their spears were broken, they fought with their swords and daggers. Some fought with weapons taken from dead Persian soldiers.

Soon only a few Greek warriors remained. They moved to a low hill. They thought the higher ground would give them an advantage. They had lost all their weapons, but they continued to fight with their hands and teeth. When the battle was over, all the Spartans and other Greek soldiers were dead. King Leonidas had been killed by several arrows. To show his victory, Xerxes ordered Leonidas' head to be cut off and put on a stake for all to see.

Leonidas and the Spartans fought bravely while facing certain death.

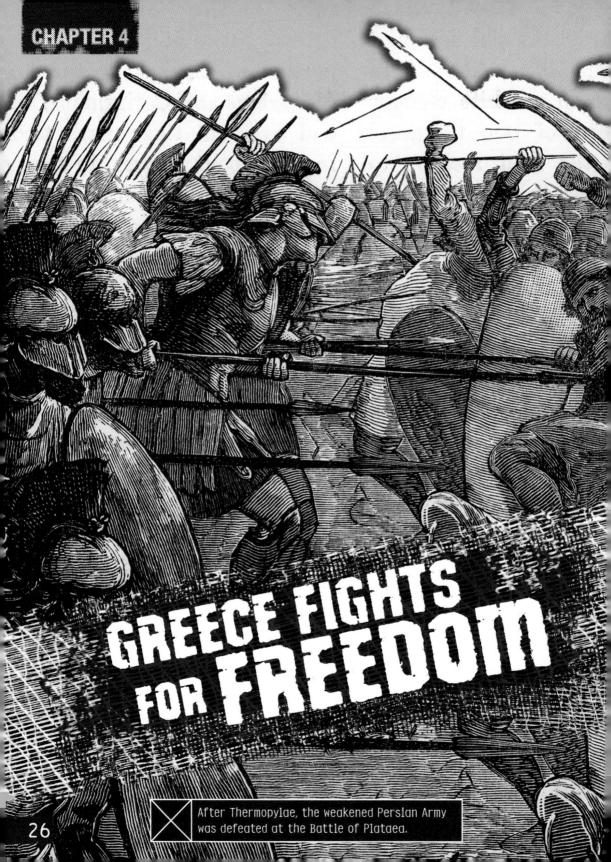

CHAPTER 4

GREECE FIGHTS FOR FREEDOM

After Thermopylae, the weakened Persian Army was defeated at the Battle of Plataea.

LEARN ABOUT

> PERSIAN CASUALTIES
> THE BATTLE OF PLATAEA
> THE SPREAD OF DEMOCRACY

Even though they lost the final battle, the 300 Spartans were regarded as heroes. They willingly fought and died against the overwhelming Persian Army. They wanted to help their country, no matter the cost.

The Persians were weakened after the battle at Thermopylae. Some historians believe the Greeks killed as many as 50,000 Persian soldiers. Xerxes was surprised the Greeks fought so hard for freedom. But he was still intent on ruling Greece. He moved his army south to continue the invasion.

The rest of Greece was inspired by the Spartans' sacrifice. The Greek Army met the Persians again at the Battle of Plataea. However, this time the Greeks had more than 100,000 troops. They defeated the Persian Army and forced them to retreat. The Persian Empire would never try to conquer Greece again.

The Dawn of Democracy

The Greeks fought the Persians to save their way of life as well as their land. The Greeks' victory over the Persians allowed Greek culture to grow. The Greeks were free to govern themselves as they pleased.

The Greeks' victory over Persia led to a time called the Classical Period. The Greeks believed in **democracy**. Soon, their ideas of independence began to spread. Other countries began forming more democratic governments.

The Greeks' beliefs in freedom are still with us today. Without the Spartans' sacrifice at Thermopylae, democratic countries might not exist as we know them today.

democracy — a form of government in which the citizens can chose their leaders

Today, a large statue of King Leonidas stands at Thermopylae to honor the sacrifice of the 300 Spartans.

ΜΟΛΟΝ ΛΑΒΕ

GLOSSARY

armor (AR-muhr) — a protective metal covering worn by ancient soldiers during combat

betray (bee-TRAY) — to do something that is not loyal and hurts someone

cavalry (KA-vuhl-ree) — soldiers who travel and fight on horseback

city-state (SI-tee STAYT) — an independent area in ancient Greece that ruled itself and had its own customs and traditions

democracy (di-MAH-kruh-see) — a form of government in which the citizens can choose their leaders

empire (EM-pyr) — a group of countries that have the same ruler

guard (GARD) — a group of soldiers who protect an important person or place

invade (in-VADE) — to send armed forces into another country in order to take it over

oracle (OR-uh-kul) — a person in ancient Greece who was believed to speak for a god

phalanx (FAY-lanks) — an ancient battle formation where soldiers overlapped their shields to create a protective wall

READ MORE

Abrams, Dennis. *Xerxes.* Ancient World Leaders. New York: Chelsea House, 2008.

Morris, Ian Macgregor. *Leonidas: Hero of Thermopylae.* Leaders of Ancient Greece. New York: Rosen, 2004.

Pearson, Anne. *Ancient Greece.* Eyewitness. New York: DK, 2007.

INTERNET SITES

FactHound offers a safe, fun way to find educator-approved Internet sites related to this book.

Here's what to do:
1. Visit www.facthound.com
2. Choose your grade level.
3. Begin your seach.

This book's ID number is 9781429622967.

FactHound will fetch the best sites for you!

INDEX